Rise Dove Awakened

DIANE EVERETT

ISBN-13: 978-1-963272-05-5

ShelteringTree.Earth, LLC Publsihing

PO Box 973, Eagle Lake, FL 33839

http://ShelteringTree.Earth

What is a "Dyslexic Friendly" Book?

Sheltering Tree Media has taken steps to make our books more friendly for those who live with dyslexia. While the following principles will not make every book readable for every reader, it is our best effort to create products that encourage reading and to support all readers.

Throughout the book, we use a font named OpenDyslexic. This is a free font that is designed to help dyslexic readers distinguish each letter from the others. For more information about OpenDyslexic, how it differs from other fonts, and research behind the font, visit their website: www.opendyslexic.com.

In our book created for adults, we use 12-point font. This size font provides the reader plenty of spacing between the letters (which is called *kerning*). The bigger, wider font tends to be easier to the reader's eyes.

The space between each word is increased (this is called *word spacing*). This helps better distinguish when one word ends and the next begins. The line spacing is greater than most common fonts (this is called *leading*). This all should help with readability.

Whenever possible, the text is Left-Aligned but it is not justified on the right side. Allowing the right side of a paragraph to remain *rough* keeps the word spacing consistent throughout.

Our Dyslexic Friendly books are printed on cream or ivory paper which is also thicker than the average book page. This minimizes the sharp contrast of black-on-white pages as well as bleedthrough of text from the previous page.

Finally, Sheltering Tree Media has made colored overlays available when you purchase a book through our online store. You can find these overlays at ShelteringTreeMedia.com/shop/dyslexic-friendly.

These are some of the principles we use to create a book as readable as possible to those living with dyslexia. Some may find this helpful; some may not. Please provide us with any insights you might have to improve our Dyslexic Friendly principles. We pray this will enable many to heighten their love for reading.

"Take what you can use, and use it.
Leave the rest".
O.C. Hunter

When I think too much
The complexities of me
Leave no room for love

Diane Everett

CONTENTS

ACKNOWLEDGEMENT

I would like to express my special thanks of gratitude to my first-grade teacher Mrs. Hurry, my friends Deborah Merta Bowen, Danielle Kimbrell, Frank Schultz, and Lili Parish. Your hours of reading, listening and discussing, praising, and correcting have made this an easy and joyous experience. Thank You

WHERE YOU SEND ME

I will send you
To a new world
Watch and observe
Learn and return the lesson
Be willing to receive
Life that is true
Experience all the good
Fear not for I am with you
Open your mind
People will question you
Tell them love
People will challenge you
Offer them truth
You have all that you need
Meet the needs of others
And grow
Now go
Be at peace
And enjoy

WITH YOUR TRUTH

I am not contending
With the differences
Between here and there
The space we occupy
As individuals
We have moved past that
Understanding unity
The one who is boundless
Indivisible
Having unified the space
Acts on unprecedented
Binding Love
I hold this truth
Smiling at the prospect
Of the next breath
Gratitude really is
All we ever needed

PERCEPTION

If the rocks that cry out
Would bring to life only praise
Then the life that men live
Will bring no less
Sun shines to heat the desert soil
And the cactus harbors water
There is an oasis inside of all
It lives inside the barren earth
It is the essence of refreshment
The holding place for the gift
That brings life to the dying
And gives meaning
To perception

BIRTH

The strength
The rhythmic necessity
The struggle relentless
The passion untamed
Throwing spheres
Into swirls
Uncontrolled by human will
Unmanned, not unaided
Calm cries
Soothing tears
An answer of compassion
That I could feel
That I could bring relief
That I could
The lessons learn
And still to be born
To give birth again

WHEN I WAS BORN

When I was born she said to me
This is your life who will you be
I sat up proudly and said with glee
This is my life I will be me

WOUNDED WARRIOR

Another wounded warrior
So tired of the fight
Relentlessly battered
No sleep through the night
Thoughts betraying thoughts
Actions that will not move
Despite my best intentions
If I can find just a little crack
In this wall I have built
Just the smallest of openings
Just enough to let a sliver of light
Into me
I stand at the doorway
Choosing the weapons of kindness
Defining the actions of this moment
To forgive in the now
To love in this minute
This precious breath of life
Incoming
That will not come ever again
To hold the present
To open my life force

With all my senses open
To receive this love
In and around and through
All that I know to be true
To stand ready
And let this wound heal

ILLUMINATION

Out of this pit I rise
Radiantly created
Waiting to know self
In awareness of what there is
Inside of me
I choose
Entering myself freely
Overcome with awe
At life-giving forces
Created for myself alone
Unique to all
Separate from none
I am becoming me

ENERGIZE ME

Fulfil the yearning of youth
The need for wandering
Exploring the nooks of nature
Where life lives freely
Deepened by the need for compassion
Abundant through the absence of fear
      Activate me
      Regenerate the desire of timeless
moments
      Where the natural walk takes place
      Without thought in movement
Full of awe
Free to express
The thrill of mind
Set on soaring planes
To rise and fall to equality
      Motivate me
      Then we will go together
      To play as children
In sunsets as the warmest colors fade to cool
In the wetness of algae dressed lily pads
In the calm swirls of reflecting water pools

WHEN I GROW UP

When I grow up
I'm goanna blow this gumdrop stand
Walk out into
The water of life
Fill my senses
With all the joy
I can hold
And bring it back to you
We can go through it together
Look at all the treasures
Hold them up to the light
And smile at each other
You will be real by then
And I will hold your hand
When I blow this gumdrop stand
And grow up

INSIDE JOB

I journeyed to Tibet today
To make a phone call to a friend
When I finally got there
All the phone lines were down
But my Spirit didn't give in
I climbed to the top of a mountain at night
And sat in the moonlight till dawn
When the sun rose above the horizon and
clouds
My reason for calling was gone

JOURNEY INSIDE

Someone must
Forge through
The misunderstood meanings
Relentlessly
Search deeper
Plummet the pit further
Into soil yet untapped
Into value unnoticed
Into life wells that spring
From unlimited source
The combination of words
Twirled into
The landscape
And sunrise
Of thought
The wonderment of the mind
Someone must explore
The cobweb caverns
Be the crusader through
Forests untamed
Father, if it be Your Will
Here I am send me

SUNDAY AFTERNOON

As they sat quietly together
The Butterfly and the Root
The root spoke to the butterfly, saying
We must take life as it comes my friend
One cannot avoid what is inevitable
And be grateful
That the God within all of us
Has the power to forgive
As we have the faith to remember
And so, they sat together quietly
On a Sunday afternoon

I AM AFRAID

What happens if I don't say
I am afraid
When the terror of the moment
Is so real that words
Cease to exist
The fear of anyone finding out
That I cannot move
Cannot respond
Compounds the anxiety
The breath of the moment
Is taken away
As I begin to release my hold
The bond to life isn't broken
It is stretched
Bouncing back with a snap
Waking me up
Peace comes in staying conscious
Through it all
Watching waiting
Participating
Each breath a choice
Knowing that each breath

Will bring back the light

Seen differently now

Through the tears in my eyes

SELF-TRUTH WALK

To walk my truth
To hold my feet firmly
On ground tilled just for me
Laboring in fields others might miss
Completing the work left undone
As time runs short of the hour
Compassion carries enough for one
While still sharing my provisions willingly
With those who pass through this field
There is not sufferance of abandonment to
self
Only a gained understanding of need
None labor in vain
None walk alone
I walk as my truth walks me

WAKE ME UP

Wake me up when this night is over
When sleep has become as restless as the day
When the nights in my dreams are full of rain
When the sunshine has gone away from the
sky
When the wind is violent
And the air is too cold to breathe
Wake me up when I have healed
Sleeping bears can slumber
Sleeping dogs with one eye open
Sleeping birds perched in their nests
Silence penetratingly beautiful silence
Stillness that comes only
When there is nothing left to study
Nothing left to believe
Nothing left to motivate
Nothing left to sustain
Nothing left to hide
Nothing left to avoid
Nothing left to process
Wake me up to new
New life it is here

New hope it is real

New love it is true

New breath let it fill me

Completely

Wake me up

Unless I sleep through the day

And miss what I have come here to understand

COOKIES THAT HEAL

And if it is too much
For a little one like me
Then I can leave
Confidently asking to be taken
Somewhere safer
Than this place of conscious confusion
Freer in spirit
Than this experience presents
I will go to God
In God's dwelling place
I will rest and heal
Laying upon healed wounds
The hurts of today
Are too deep
The human flesh
Of this dimension
Still soft and pink
From the last healing
Now, below the surface
I see the vastness of injury
Not the weightiness
But the width and depth

Not a burden
Knowing there is
No other place to go
Encompassed by a golden light
A lucid fluidity
A shield of protection
My Spirit self
Clearing and cleaning the obscurity
Of vague and misshapen beliefs
Humanness that brought such sorrow
I will sit in my Father's lap
And eat cookies
Until I am full and satisfied
My Father will hold me
While my Mother
Takes my hands in Her own
And reminds me who I am
When I know the purity of love
When I feel the healing of understanding
Compassion now balanced and harmonic
My Mother Father God presence
Always watching and guiding
I take in the breath of Love
My voice becomes
The power of this moment

I speak Yes
To the open door
Of freedom
Of love
Of clarity
This child of God made healthy
Will go out and play again
With the voice of healing
That says, "Thank you."

Diane Everett

CARRY ME

I carry my world within me
In images great and small
A world that is created
By answering life's sweet call
I look outside my window eyes
Surveying all I see
And take the parts that sparkle
Back inside with me
To hold them up to brighter light
The worlds light is to dim
To see if what I gathered
Is of muck or crystal gem
It takes a lot of work you know
To build a world and watch it grow
To keep it in proportion
The way that God would do
God gives me strength and loving power
To know just what to choose
God teaches me in simple ways
To gain and not to lose
And when God bids me follow
I quicken on my way

And ask if God will carry me
Again throughout today

NEED INK

I always wanted a poet's perspective
To be inside the box
Examining the inner wall
Or outside on the most corner point
Standing diagonally taking notes
The pen and I don't always agree
We fight to get the ideas on paper
Maybe my problem is really with the paper
Maybe the problem is with me
I question what a poet's perspective might be
To see if I fit
This misfit peg in a round hole
Struggling always to get the message out
Which is after all the point
To form for myself the idea
To draw for you my word pictures
I call my name from within
To see if I will answer
Perhaps I call to test if I can hear
And still I want a poet's perspective
To be inside or outside the box
Whether deaf or hearing

To know that the problem is me

Which is after all the solution

And still prove that I fit

To struggle and define

And in this end

Still I want a poet's perspective

NO TRESPASSING

You dare to take the harvest
From fields that you do not own
You believe that you are able
To overpower another
And take that which belongs to another
You will have no part of my meal
The fruit I eat is sweet
Grown from my own delights
Tilled on my own soil
Harvested with my own labor
The rain that nurtures me
Falls from my own tears
Collected from the many years
That I have worked and planted
This is the wealth that I have
This is the reward that I yield
This is the pleasure that I delight in
This is mine
All that I see
Within the visions of my world
As for your trespass
I will not delay you

You are free to move on

No longer welcome here

No longer free to rest in these meadows

No longer allowed to eat from these trees

Their fruit is better suited to fall and decay

And begin again than to fill the belly

Of an unwanted visitor

You will continue as you will

Until a time when

You are no longer able

The memory of you

Will be caught up in the wind

And chased away

I have found no regret

A MOMENT

I took a moment of stillness
In a day of hurry
I just wanted one more
Moment still in the heart of Peace
Quiet in the presence of Love
Lightness rising
Like a Dove who rises
To greet the day
I have risen
Held
Loved
Known
The Peace
That dwells within
This moment of stillness

GOD LOVES ME

When as a child I go to God
I know that I'm set free
To do the best that I can do
Be the best that I can be
In weakness when I think
That I have learned all that I can
Life sets before me struggles
God gives me strength to understand
As the tears of my repentance flow
Love washes clean my inner glow
I look beyond my weakness
As I give God back control
I know that I might never have
The words to praise God's name
But forever I'll be grateful
That God loves me just the same

I AM THE MOVIE

I found a plan
In my back right hip pocket
Then I got my plan back
I took a step forward
And a little to the left
Then I got my step back
Yea, ok then, I did put
A little ass in my walk
Then I got my sense of humor back
And in this moment
This very life filling breath
I got my love back
It really is so very simple
I also almost missed it
I almost looked away for a moment
Then I got my vision back
And realization struck me
In the forehead like a brick
I watch myself, and you, and others
I breathe
I watch my movie
Then I get my life back

SPARKLES

Safe at last
A new freedom
To just be me
To love and live
Inside this very precious
Bubble of personal space
I fill it all up
Move from one side to the other
Watch my feet move
Wave my arms way up to the top
And bow down
My knees bent
Touch the ground beneath me
Breathe
Slowly steadfast
Intentional
Holding space for myself
My energy grows
Light illuminates
My personal space
I feel my glow
As I wear my sparkles on my skin
Where I end and you begin.

IDENTITY

That I would know myself and all my parts

Taste again the colors; wash in the feelings of
the rainbow

Know the shapes and sounds as they dance in
the air

Wake up again

To hear the words spoken

Yes, to me, spoken to me

No longer broken

No longer defeated

Not doubting

Wake me up and I awaken

Knowing the truth that stands firm within as
well as without

My torn down walls

My tangible reality

This just a beginning but nevertheless

I have begun

PAUSED AND MUSING

I smiled at my name today
I saw it in print
I've seen it before
And recognized
Myself in it
Written out in letters
Of an alphabet
In a language of words
A first
A middle
A last
So much like my life
Looking out to the horizon
While standing vertically
So deep the light goes
So far below
The language of words
My smile rising above
Almost formless
Without scrutiny spinning
More of a beam
Than a smile

Smiles are limited

To the face

 A beam is boundless

How funny

All of this

From a name on a page

Written out in letters

of an alphabet

in a language

of words

That causes me to smile

FILLING THE VOID

So beautiful
Your yellow intuitive manners
Flowing into the green
Of your heart space
From your high place
Angel wings against the sky
Centered in the eye of love
You see me and all around me
I am centered in your smile
My innocence plays in front of you
Calling for you to join the fun
Laugh with the wind
And giggle at the sunbeams
That tickle the skin in softness
Your sigh moves the barrier between us
And for a moment a dim vale is lifted
Transparent to the illusion of time and space
We fill the void of life
With the matter of laughing smiles and
heartfelt hugs
The appreciation of life lived abundantly
The joy of life's breath

Holding in this moment of perfection

The divinity we share

The captivation of purity

The smiling glow of awakened souls

MOTHER TO CHILD

Mother:
Gently, so quietly
Hush child, hush
Struggles will come
Then gently go
Open your pretty eyes
Little one, precious one
Life is for living
Now, off you go
Child:
But I haven't learned
How to live and I fear
That I won't make it
Out there on my own
Mother:
Think of your question
Then answer it slowly
What do you see in life
Frightening you so
Haven't you seen
That with questions come answers

Mother continued:
With sorrow comes new joy
With dawn comes the day
Haven't you witnessed
With every beginning
We gather our strength
Though tossed by a storm
True love does not sway
And if, in your answer
A Yes, you are chiding
Then perhaps it's not life
That is frightening you
But a deeper dilemma
A trust not yet wakened
That in order to live
You must find your own question
You must feel your own sorrow
You must start your own day
You must have your own knowing
And strength through the seasons
You must find your own love
And prove it won't sway

Child:

Yes, I am willing
To face life and live it
Yes, I am willing to enter today
And somehow I know
That with this understanding
There really is not fear
To stand in my way
So gently and quietly
I will be leaving now
Please watch me enter
This new life calling me
And if, in the process
A part is found dying

Child continued:

May it be the part needing

To stay here with you

May it be the part lacking

The faith to find true love

The part found in freedom

That would slow this child down

The part that won't understand

Truth found in reason

That sees life's distractions

As only a sound

The part that won't give up

The anger it's holding

The part that rebels

At the thought of new day

Though it's witnessed

That life is the answer

And Love is the way

WHERE I AM

I am here
I am worthy
I have looked
Searched
Discovered and
Walked away from
This place where you are
Where you live
And dwell
And have being
I just want to stay here
With You
Now
And you say
I am here
And I say
I don't want to leave again
And struggle and strive to come back
I tend to wander
Or get sidetracked
And then I get lost
I get lost in so many beauties

So boundless

Without space or time

So loving

And my legs get shaky

I look and yell out

(Probably in your ear)

Then you touch me

And I know where you are

You are here

I breathe

I am here

I am worthy

I need you

To be here

Where I am

WHERE THE THOUGHTS GO

Where do the thoughts go
When you're done thinking them
Do they run down a tunnel
Do they crawl in a hole
Do they float up to heaven
And get caught by your soul
Do they make the sun brighter
Bring light from your eyes
Do they leave this earthly body
And fly up into the sky
All the precious mumble sounds
Like words that make this world go around
We know that they are substance
There are thoughts that ride a bus
There are other thoughts that we'd prefer
Were not inside of us
We bend them and we box them
Even put some out of sight
We corral them and control them
Sometimes with great delight
We move them and we mold them
And we form them into shape

If we really pay attention
Then none of them escape
So, do thoughts go where we tell them
And compel them up and down left or right
Or are they moved by a current much deeper
Than a thought in a forest groove
I think they dance with Spirit
And by Spirits love are moved

QUANTUM MEDITATION BREATHS

One is for fun

With your arms love me

Bright and Shiny

Light within hold me

Small and simple I smile

With your voice breathe into me

Truth and Peace

Silence within listen to me

Quiet and still I smile

You give me Light and Love

You give me Truth and Peace

You give me Life Peaceful and True

You smile at me and I smile

Two is for Shoe

Snowflake

She knows your design

Unique each of You

Every frozen cell

United

Balanced

Perfect

Harmonically bound
Sunlight dances on your back
Every delightful light beam
A Peaceful Presence
As you are melted
By the warmth of Her love
And become a part
Of the White Canvas of Her Light

Three is for Tree

I raise my arms to the sky
Embracing all I see
My arms reach up beyond their stretch
Just like a mighty tree
A tree whose limbs reach upward
With equal roots below
A mighty fortress of God's love
A face the Oak will grow

Four is for Core

I reach for more
A birthright to be all
I bring to me
From the
Lower

Middle

Upper

Dan Tien

By the grace of love and light

I bring back the birthright

To be the best me I can be

To reach my highest human potential

Filled with source

The boundlessness of Spirit

The abundance of an infinite core

I am

ONE DAY

Set the sequence
Of perfectly timed rhythms
Climb to the higher side
With hinds feet
All four feet together
See the mornings blazing sun
Adjusting your sight
To the colors within you
Here and now be present
So that the peace that brings you wisdom
And the peace that overcomes
Brings you love and light and wonderment
As your work today is done
Go to sleep and make no mention
Of the sorrows this day held
Only know that love surrounds you
In the truth that all is well
Climb up to the highest peak
And absorb the luminous glow
Feel loves presence all around you
Ask for knowledge and you'll know
You're a precious jewel of light my love

As you own the path that brought you
To this lofty mountain view
Owning life lived fully
Is what you are here to do
As you learn to love another
Bringing love to full return
Bless the lessons you will teach
And the lessons you will learn

ABOUT THE AUTHOR

Diane Everett lives in central Florida. She started writing in the first grade and told Mrs. Hurry her first grade teacher that someday she was going to write a book. When she isn't writing or working in the IST field, she is an accomplished Outsider Artist creating award-winning Root Art.

Rise Dove Awakened is a book of inspiring awareness of where one person fits in this world. A collection of poems revealing a journey from me to we, the joy of self-discovery written as uplifting and passionate poetry hoping to bring the reader from an individual perspective of life to the humanness of our collective sense of self. It is the first in a series of metaphysical and visionary poetry by Ms. Everett.

DISCUSSION GUIDE
for Book Clubs, Journaling,
or Personal Contemplation

1. What personal lessons did you find in the poems that will bring you to a better understanding of yourself?

2. What poems do you relate to that hold the attitude of finding peace in accepting yourself as you are?

3. In what authentic way did you identify with the writer in any of these poems. How did you relate?

4. Who was narrating, the poets inner writer or the poet waking up? Give an example.

5. What did you see in these poems that would cause anyone to change? What was the poet's biggest motivation to change? What motivates you to change?

6. What would have happened if the poet had not come to an understanding of her connection with God? How might that have changed the course of someone's life?

7. Which poem helped most to look at your own conflict and seek a solution? What resolutions have you come to after reading this book?

8. How were the places described in these poems relatable?

9. Would the poet have woken up and risen without overcoming the obstacles identified in these poems?

10. What attitude change in the poet caused the biggest change in your own values?

11. What did you see as the author's most conflicted idea?

12. Which poem caused you the most personal conflict and how will you resolve it?

13. What was the poem that caused you to see a different point of view? With what poem did you best identify?

14. What was your initial gut feeling when you saw the cover of the book? Did the Dove Rise Awakened?

15. In what way did the ideas and concepts written about in these poems instill in you a need to be better at something or change the way you view growing into a better moral design of yourself?

16. How can you relate to the Dove? What poem best reflects your identification?

17. Do the poems flow in a way that encourages support in becoming authentic and whole emotionally and or spiritually?

18. What is there in your own search for your best self that responds to these poems and makes you want to keep reading?

19. How would you compare the energy at the beginning of the book and then again toward the end?

20. What was the turning point in the poems from being centered in self to being centered in God?

21. What poems did you feel were most authentic?

22. Which poems have the ending you had expected? Which poems were the most satisfying emotionally and spiritually?

23. What would you like to see in a second book of poetry by the author of these poems?

24. What was the most beneficial experience you have had as a result of these poems?

SHELTERING
TREE
●
EARTH
PUBLISHING

We are an exclusive traditional publishing house.

Our readers, once they finish one of our books, will be able to get up and face the world wiser, stronger, centered, and with the assurance that we are not alone: we are all a part of the Sheltering Tree on Earth.

If you as a writer feel that same calling, please refer to

www.ShelteringTree.Earth

www.ingramcontent.com/pod-product-compliance
Lightning Source LLC
Chambersburg PA
CBHW032215040426
42449CB00005B/602